This book belongs to :

....

Welcome Friends!

We've come from all
around the world
just to meet you!

ARCTIC

AFRICA

AUSTRALIA

monkey

lion

zebra

hippopotamus

cheetah

rhinoceros

giraffe

meerkat

elephant

seal

penguin

snow leopard

polar bear

snowy owl

reindeer

koala bear

kangaroo

platypus

Thank you
See you soon!

The

Featured

Elements

GIFT CO.

Made in the USA
Coppell, TX
27 February 2020